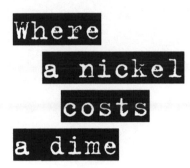

Where
a nickel
costs
a dime

Where a nickel costs a dime

by willie perdomo

W. W. Norton & Company   New York   London

The text of this book is composed in Bell Centennial
with the display set in Trixie Cameo
Composition by ComCom, Inc.
Manufacturing by The Courier Companies, Inc.
Book design by Guenet Abraham

Library of Congress Cataloging-in-Publication Data

Perdomo, Willie.
Where a nickel costs a dime / by Willie Perdomo.
p.   cm.
ISBN 0-393-31383-2 (pbk.)
1. City and town life—New York (N.Y.)—Poetry.   2. Puerto
Ricans—New York (N.Y.)—Poetry.   I. Title
PS3566.E691216W48   1996
811'.54—dc20   95-13225

W. W. Norton & Company, Inc., 500 Fifth Avenue, New York, N.Y. 10110
W. W. Norton & Company Ltd., 10 Coptic Street, London WC1A 1PU

2 3 4 5 6 7 8 9 0

para mi madre Carmen

for being the mother & father

perdoname madre mia

for the nights you cried to sleep

while Papo was falling . . .

And . . .
con amor
para Ree-Ree
who on a rainy October morning
let a skinny Puerto Rican kid
into her Harlem brownstone
and gave him the world

Shout out to
the believers
and disbelievers—

ONE LOVE . . .

Uptown on Lenox Avenue

Where a nickel costs a dime

LANGSTON HUGHES

Contents

Where
a nickel
costs
a dime

123rd Street Rap

A day on
123rd Street

goes a little
something like
this:

Automatic bullets bounce
off stoop steps

It's about time to pay
all my debts

Church bells bong for
drunken mourners

Baby men growing on
all the corners

Money that
ain't mine

Sun that
don't shine

Trees that
don't grow

Wind that
won't blow

Drug posses
ready to rumble

Ceilings starting
to crumble

Abuelas close
eyes and pray

While they watch
the children play

Not much I
can say

Except day turns
to night

And I can't tell what's
wrong from what's right

on 123rd Street

Because she liked the "kind of music" that I listened to and she liked the way I walked as well as the way I talked, she always wanted to know where I was from.

If I said that I was from 110th Street and Lexington Avenue, right in the heart of a transported Puerto Rican town, where the hodedores live and night turns to day without sleep, do you think then she might know where I was from?

Where I'm from, Puerto Rico stays on our minds when the fresh breeze of café con leche y pan con mantequilla comes through our half-open windows and under our doors while the sun starts to rise.

Where I'm from, babies fall asleep to the bark of a German shepherd named Tarzan. We hear his wandering footsteps under a midnight sun. Tarzan has learned quickly to ignore the woman who begs her man to stop slapping her with his fist. "Please, baby! Por favor! I swear it wasn't me. I swear to my mother. Mameeee!!" (Her dead mother told her that this would happen one day.)

Where I'm from, Independence Day is celebrated every day. The final gunshot from last night's murder is followed by the officious knock of a warrant squad coming to take your bread, coffee and freedom away.

Where I'm from, the police come into your house without knocking. They throw us off rooftops and say we slipped. They shoot my father and say he was crazy. They put a bullet in my head and say they found me that way.

Where I'm from, you run to the hospital emergency room because some little boy spit a razor out of his mouth and carved a crescent into your face. But you have to understand, where I'm from even the dead have to wait until their number is called.

Where I'm from, you can listen to Big Daddy retelling stories on his corner. He passes a pint of light Bacardi, pouring the dead's tributary swig onto the street. "I'm God when I put a gun to your head. I'm the judge and you in my courtroom."

Where I'm from, it's the late night scratch of rats' feet that explains what my mother means when she says slowly, "Bueno, mijo, eso es la vida del pobre." (Well, son, that is the life of the poor.)

Where I'm from, it's sweet like my grandmother reciting a quick prayer over a pot of hot rice and beans. Where I'm from, it's pretty like my niece stopping me in the middle of the street and telling me to notice all the stars in the sky.

Nigger-Reecan Blues

—Hey, Willie. What are you, man? Boricua? Moreno? Que? Are you
   Black? Puerto Rican?
—I am.
—No, silly. You know what I mean: What are you?
—I am you. You are me. We the same. Can't you feel our veins
   drinking the same blood?

   —But who said you was a Porta-Reecan?
   —Tu no ere Puerto Riqueño, brother.
   —Maybe Indian like Ghandi-Indian?
   —I thought you was a Black man.
   —Is one of your parents white?
   —You sure you ain't a mix of something like Cuban and
   Chinese?
   —Looks like an Arab brother to me.
   —Naahhh, nah, nah . . . You ain't no Porty-Reecan.
   —I keep tellin' y'all: That boy is a Black man with an accent.

If you look real close you will see that your spirits are standing right
next to our songs. Yo soy Boricua! Yo soy Africano! I ain't lyin'. Pero
mi pelo is kinky y curly y mi skin no es negro pero it can pass . . .

   —Hey, yo. I don't care what you say. You Black.

I ain't Black! Every time I go downtown la madam blankita de
Madison Avenue sees that I'm standing next to her and she holds her
purse just a bit tighter. Cabdrivers are quick to turn on their
Off-Duty signs when they see my hand in the air. And the
newspapers say that if I'm not in front a gun you can bet I'll be
behind one. I wonder why . . .

—Cuz you Black, nigger!

Don't call me no nigger. I am not Black, man. I had a conversation
with my professor and it went just like this:
"So, Willie, where are you from?"
"I'm from Harlem."
"Ohhh . . . Are you Black, Willie?"
"No, but we all the same and—"
"Did you know our basketball team is nationally ranked?"

—Te lo estoy diciendo, brother. Ese hombre es un moreno.
Miralo!

Mira, pana mia, yo no soy moreno! I just come out of Jerry's Den and
the coconut spray on my new shape-up is smelling fresh all the way
up 125th Street. I'm lookin' slim and I'm lookin' trim and when my
compai Davi saw me he said: "Coño, Papo, te parece como un
moreno, pana. Word up, kid, you look just like a light-skin moreno."

—What I told you? You Black my brother.

Damn! I ain't even Black and here I am suffering from the young
Black man's plight / the old white man's burden / and I ain't even
Black, man / a Black man I am not / Boricua I am / ain't never really
was / Black / like me . . .

—Y'all leave that boy alone. He got what they call the
"nigger-reecan blues."

I'm a spic! I'm a nigger!
Spic! Spic! Just like a nigger.

Neglected, rejected, oppressed and dispossessed
From banana boats to tenements
Street gangs to regiments
Spic, spic, spic. I ain't nooooo different than a nigger!

Too tired
for words

you say
give me

life I
love you

like always
I return all

the kisses you
blow my way

I can see
dry tears

at the bottom
of your hollow

cheeks I
heard you cried

twice today
once when the

sun came out and
Carlito didn't give

you the ten
dollars he promised

you for your wake
up and then you

cried real tears when
one of the guys gave

Machito five
dollars if he dared

to ask you to suck
his those were

real tears I saw too
tired for words I

say give me
life I love

you when you
return all the kisses

I blow
your way

bop gone bad

lips chapped
and pink
from too much
jazz and drink

corners of your
mouth sag from all
that rap and scag

no hat tilted to
the side or a bop
on every stride

will make you look
as cool as you
use to be

Take Out

Hmmm, I said, when I saw the neon menu on the walls of Wong's Chinese Foods. He must be doing good. I remember there were just big black and white handwritten signs for sales on rib-tips and green bananah. Shit seems to happen all of a sudden and all of a sudden a marked police car stopped in front of the joint. One officer stood in the car while the other, McLary was his name, 9026 was his number, stepped into the take-out, hand on his glock, ready to order. Officer in the car was staring into the rearview mirror looking for one last collar, sure that somebody on the corner was dirty. And then that's when two tragedies were relayed over the radio while the beef & broccoli was jugglin' in the wok. Staticstaticstaticstatic . . . WHITE FEMALE ASSAULTED AND ROBBED NEAR THE 125TH STREET METRO-NORTH TRAIN STATION. SUSPECTS WERE LAST SEEN RUNNING EAST TOWARD THE WILLIS AVENUE BRIDGE. HISPANIC TEENS, ONE WITH A YANKEE BASEBALL CAP AND THE OTHER WITH A GOLD TOOTH. USE CAUTION AS BOTH SUSPECTS ARE SAID TO BE ARMED. Staticstaticstatic . . . GUNSHOTS FIRED NEAR THE SOUTHEAST ENTRANCE TO THE CARVER HOUSING PROJECTS. ONE FATAL SHOT CONFIRMED. HISPANIC, 18 YEARS OLD, ONE ANGEL TORRES A.K.A. "BLONDIE." CAUTION IS ADVISED UPON ENTRY. "Oh shit, officer!" I say grabbing my shrimp foo young and running out Wong's toward Carver Projects. "That's my cousin."

Mmmm . . . those glazed donuts from Georgie's smell like they just
    came out the oven.
A breeze of fresh collard-greens bum-rushes me from the open
    doors of Soul Food Haven.
Damn— I'm hungry . . .
Scent of indigo incense caresses me into a dream of kings and
    queens.
Manchild steppin' strong on the street with his fresh-out-the-box
    Nike 380s,
Holdin' his head high he plexes his gold Nefertiti medallion.
Curling irons are pressing kitchen away,
And the history of Black hair is changing every day.
Bob Marley's self-determination blasting out of totally
    Rasta-owned AWARENESS RECORDS,
Martin's dream making my hair stand,
And Malcolm up the block telling me to hit back if I really wanna be
    free.
PUBLIC ENEMY bringing the noise.
Little queen in her stroller points to the discount toys.
Homemade Kid Capri tapes at high black market prices cuz they
    boomin'
Wanna make a donation to the nation, brother?
A fight! A fight!
A moreno and his hermano—again?
Did you hear the pow! boom! plah!
Guns or drums? Take your pick.
Skunk weed is all I need to forget what I gotta do and why.
Love starin' at me with a sly smile.
Senegalese masks hanging off parking lot gates,
A laugh sits next to a cry: the face of tragedy straight from the
    motherland.

We can't wear all them 8-Ball jackets on display at Dr. Jay's.
One man blues band—SATAN
Steady jammin' by the Studio Museum of Harlem
I go from a hip-hop strut to a blues rut
Now—let me ask you somethin':
Did you hear all that while you was walking up 125th Street?
Did you see all that while you was walkin' up 125th Street?
Did you feel all that while you was walkin' up 125th Street?
Or was you just on your way
to pay
the phone bill?

Sangre en Harlem

You seen that movie
SANGRE EN HARLEM?
Blood in Harlem
starring some kid named Miguel
or some kid named José
or some kid named Kareem
or some kid named Daryl
or some kid . . .

Bloods are blue in the face
by the time Homicide arrives
The stage has been set for
me to die once again

Blood is blue in the night
filling the cracks in the street
All the props are real
After they bag me up
the bullets will keep singing

Next to the theater
street photographers
give lovers a chance
to freeze their romance
for five dollars you get
black velvet backdrops
French phones &
straw thrones

An old lady in the audience squeezes her grandson against her
    bosom. Her tears fell a long time ago.

Unemployed Mami

Even though she don't have a job mami still works hard.
The last twenty-three years of her life haven been spent
teaching a poet and killing generations of cockroaches
with sky-blue plastic slippers, t.v. guides, and pink tissues.
She prays for the poet as he runs into the street looking
for images of Boricua sweetness to explode in his face.
The young roaches escape in the dark while my unemployed
mami goes to sleep cursing at them.

Even though she don't have a job mami still works hard.
She walked behind my drunken father, in the rain, as he
stumbled into manhood and oblivion in America wearing
his phony mambo king pinky ring. He beat my mami,
he beat my mami, stop beating my mami! with the black
umbrella; the one with the fake ivory horsehead handle.
I still hear the same salsa blaring out the same social club
where I use to fall asleep and dream happy lives.

Even though she don't have a job mami still works hard.
Every year she prays for my abuela who died in a sweet
bed of Holy Water y Ben Gay while the poet was kicking
his mother inside her stomach. Mami looks at Miss America,
Miss Universe, Miss Everything, every year and then she runs
into her bedroom to dig out her high school yearbook from
underneath her pile of "important papers." "Look, Papo.
Look at your mother when she was eighteen years old. She
was pretty like those girls on t.v." You still are, I say.

Even though she don't have a job mami still works hard.
Lately, she plays slow songs of lost love over and over and
over. She looks out the window only when it rains, measuring

tear drops against the rain drops. Where is that man, I wonder,
as I sit in my room writing and rewriting a poem for her.
I catch her peeking at me from the corner of her eye, wondering if
I do, I really do, love you and that's not the record, that's me, I say,
hugging her with a kiss.

Don't cry, mami.
Even though you don't have a job
I know you still be working hard.

Song for Langston

I sang all night
And cried all day

Been waitin' for a
Storm to come my way

Drown the tears
Make soft the pain

I hope my prayers
Are not in vain

He rubbed his temples as if to say, Damn, I can't believe it, again. Why me? No cans to kick, no bottles to throw, no puddles of dirty water to spit in and shatter what you see—just mad because it's Friday night and the courts are closed for the weekend.

The long letters start to pile up on my desk. He gained weight, drug-free plans to get a G.E.D. so he could find a job when the board releases him. "All that druggin' fucked my head up. I wasn't thinkin' right." I know all of this without opening the envelopes.

A man's vision becomes clear when looking through bars or over barbed-wire gates. In the afternoon he wishes he could fly so he could be down with the flock that flies above the yard during lunch time.

I let the final slam of steel doors on the lock-up answer my letters. Lights out and he's laying on his bed thinkin' about what we doin', Friday night in El Barrio and love and death are standing on the corner, smiling at you.

Brother Lo

A barefoot Brother Lo
came out his hole in the wall
and jumped onto the top of the
blue mailbox on the corner.

He yanked a palm full of strands
from his thick black beard and blew
them against the breeze that warned
of rain.

He stretched his mighty arms toward the
sky and shouted his daily prophecy to the
boys standing near the mailbox, listening to
music, drinking beer.

> "Go 'head. Laugh at me. Y'all spend all
> day laughing and selling that shit. But
> I ain't got no time to joke. I speak the
> truth. The sky is ready to open and rain
> fire. Nothin' but ashes gonna be left where
> y'all standing."

One boy drank a long swig and said:

> "Let it rain. But you better put on some shoes
> before the sky opens cuz your feet stink, Brother
> Lo. They kickin' like Bruce Lee when he's mad!"

A loose Chihuahua ran away from his owner and
let off a nervous bark. Brother Lo leaped off the
mailbox and dashed through the schoolyard. A
congregation of born-again Christians were walking
home, singing hymns for our salvation, pressing their
leather Bibles against their hearts.

Brother Lo laughed like thunder having fun. A Metro-North train was roaring on the elevated tracks, rushing out of Harlem toward New Haven.

No one heard
the sky open.

Revolution

One night
Brother Lo told
Officer Rooney:

> Muthafucka
> take off your
> badge and gun
> and see if I don't
> bust your ass all
> the way back to
> the precinct.

in case
of an
emergency

call a
cop

but make
sure

you cop
your cure

before you
call—

quick!

Last Junkie Poem

The last poem I write
about a junkie
will be the one
he steals
as I ride the bus
early in the afternoon
from the east side
to the west side

Hair like Medusa's
he stops in a barbershop
strolling his dusty 19 inch
on a ricketyrackety stroller
rusting at the wheels:

>"Black and white t.v.
>Baby stroller
>You got a baby, baby?
>I'll give you the t.v. for free."

Bus vrrrooommms past Levin's Drugstore.
Look! A honey-hue cutie skipping into the
library. Halfaday in Harlem and her thighs
are thick, knees knocking under her black
and blue plaid skirt. She probably one of
them goody-good rich girls from Hamilton
Terrace is what the bad boy in the Yankee
baseball cap said, ready to roll three green
dice against the church wall.

>*five he four better*
>*ten he don't*

I got ten
ten in it

Fingers snap a wooo-
ooohhh she bad roll
one day, boy
one day
she gonna
be mine

Head crack, baby!
Drop all that cream . . .

Somebody yells for a girl named Nee-Cee.
Nee-Cee! Nee-Cee!
Dashing into the Dominican deli,
passing the schoolgirl,
hot-pink fake leather slippers starting to peel
on the concrete.
The sun don't shine for that girl no more . . .
No one knows her secret like the old man
who promised her bubble gum—all she had to do
was follow him to the roof so he could show her his bird kingdom.
Ask the old man what happened and he'll say:
I ain't have nothin' but hard dick and bubble gum and I was fresh
        outta bubble gum.

Running out the deli with a carton of milk
cradled in her arms,
first Newport of the day
dangling from her lips,
Nee-Cee wants to know what moves me to my notepad.

Love poems?
Sheeet . . .
Love poems don't pay the rent.
Love poems don't pay for the milk.
Can't eat no love poems.
Gotta come stronger than that, baby.

Before my stop I see the last poem
of the day.
It's about the jazz heads
feeding the pigeons in front of the clinic.
Monk and Miles
playing on their tape recorders
while they sip Thunderbird and Kool-Aid
outta five-cent plastic cups.
Same group meets in Marcus Garvey Park
which use to be called Mount Morris Park.
Malcolm X Boulevard use to be Lenox Avenue.
Adam Clayton Powell Boulevard use to be 7th Avenue.
Frederick Douglass Boulevard use to be 8th Avenue.
Martin Luther King Boulevard use to be 125th Street.
There's a new consciousness in the air,
but this group will be the first to tell you:

> *Just cuz you change the name,*
> *It sure don't change the game.*

Some of them
won't be there tomorrow
after the bilingual monster
AIDS

SIDA
comes for them—
But the music will stay
just like their rap,
check it:

"These young boys think they own the world. Looking like clowns
with all that fake gold hanging from their necks. Shittin' where they
eat, driving crazy through the street, playing that loud stupid shit. I
be speaking to God every night and I be tellin' him that tomorrow's
light looks kinda bleak."

This is true
I say as I step off
the m101
with the last poem I write
about a junkie.

Looking for happy endings
we came
over-extended familias
with secrets named
sofrito y salsa
that made broken homes smell
good from the outside
that made you run up the stairs
three steps at a time
Even third generation
Africans from North Carolina
started using Goya beans

Signs of life
were up on the wall
NO LOITERING
NO RADIO PLAYING
NO SELLING DRUGS
NO TRESPASSING
NO SMOKING

We came to this skyscraped city
to live
to survive
to die
in concentration camps
named after
dead presidents
dead abolitionists
dead peanut farmers
whose names have no meaning

as we pray
and sing
in a night lit by candles
using
healing herbs
magic potions
to save the souls
of our children
who run hard and fast
looking for themselves

Number halls
behind bodegas
next to casitas
by botanicas
keep history
on the same block
Cuchifrito kitchens
can't compete
with take-out
chicken wing dynasties
because they don't accept
food stamps

On the second Sunday in June
you can watch us on Channel 11
parading down an avenue
that doesn't belong to us
singing a celebration of an island
that some of us will never see

We
Boricuas
Porta-Rocks
Spics
Goya-bean-eatin'-muthafu—
us was the first
to come in planes
no chains
just one-way tickets
to a sold-out dream

In order to understand
the pain and joy of all this
you must listen to Pancho
crouched low on the corner
refusing to learn English
singing the last song he
heard before he got on
the plane to New York

Prophet Born in Harlem

for James Baldwin

Never trust
a man
who comes
to you
with cock
tales and
smiles

Begging to
give you
diamonds for
your ohhh so
talented self

Strip the mask
off his face
until you see
blood pour
like yours

Talk about
the real problem

And don't be
scared to use
four letter words:

L-O-V-E

It works better than
a bullet

baby

Que Viva Chango

Que viva chango
Que viva chango
> Dona Rosa kept praying into the black
> crucifix clenched between her palms

Que viva chango
Que viva chango
> Morena was calling the evil spirit
> blowing cigar smoke into all the rooms
> telling the spirit that it was too weak to
> fight with her

Que viva chango
Que viva chango
> Pancha was sweeping the floor with a coconut.
> I know you, she said to me. I sat silent watching
> Junito who was lying on the floor, wiping chalk
> dust out of his eyes.

Que viva chango
Que viva chango
> Morena finally caught the spirit.
> She gouged out its eyes, pulled its hair out,
> stripped the skin off its back and drowned it in
> a large sifter of Holy Water and light rum.

Que viva chango
Que viva chango
> After Pancha finished outlining Junito's body, she
> wrapped him up in a white bed sheet and crumpled
> the remaining chalk along its perimeter. She chanted.
> And chanted. And chanted. No more harm could be
> done to Junito.

Que viva chango

Que viva chango

> Morena clapped three times and blew smoke toward
> me. She said, "I know you, too. You're the one who
> leaves before danger comes. Your saint comes to
> whisper in your ear. It tells you to go home."

Que viva chango

Que viva chango

> Scared because she was right, I got up, ready to leave.
> Yesterday, after I left the spot, some kids tried to kill
> Junito while I was upstairs looking at t.v.

Save the Youth

I can only speak about
the youth
growing on the corners
of my block
like weeds
in an abandoned lot

Racing in fast lanes
to grab all the loot
Living lifestyles of the
rich and dangerous
No time to buy dreams
or call confession lines

Smoking blunts of buddha
and making Tony Montana decisions
They empathize
with his rise
and celebrate his fall into
the fountain of his world

You see—
if you gonna die
that's how
you do it
Paid in full
with your balls
in place
a stone face
and shooting back
Definitely shooting
back

I can only speak about
the youth
growing on the corners
of my block
like weeds in an
abandoned lot

They stay up
way past bed time
selling brand-name poison
keeping the economy healthy
and making new rules

Just like the men
who built
this country

Clyde

No one in the building has heard Clyde say a word in the last ten years. I say hi to him every morning on my way to work. He just nods, smokes his cigarette butts, and says, "Uh-hm, huh."

Ms. Mason collects Clyde's Social Security checks and uses them to buy school clothes for her grandchildren. She told my mother that Clyde use to be a nice, clean-cut, Christian boy. But one morning he found his mother naked with her head in the oven. He stopped talking ever since that morning.

Gee-Man who stands on the stoop all day long smoking reefer and drinking beer, talks to Clyde. Gee-Man thinks he's always right. He said Clyde smoked so much angel dust that he just forgot how to talk. That's it. Gee-Man also said that Clyde was no joke when it came to playing some ball. "Tell 'em, Clyde. They couldn't fuck with you on the basketball court, back in the day." Clyde just nods, smokes his cigarette butts, and says, "Uh-hm, huh."

During the winter, Clyde sleeps on the fifth floor after the Housing Police finish their rounds. All the tenants bring Clyde leftover food and summer clothes. The kids make fun of Clyde. They play tag throughout the building, yelling, screaming and slamming the doors. They pour cold water on Clyde while he sleeps and offer him a comb for his afro. Sometimes they pull his pants down and yell "the crack!" I tell the kids to stop making all that noise because Clyde might have something to say one day. He got to have something to say: we all need someone to speak to, living so close to each other, fenced in by brick walls, gates, police, that sometimes we shout and curse at each other all night long. So I know Clyde got something to say.

It was the first time I saw Edwin wearing a suit. It was the first time I
saw Chino cry. Set up by his right-hand man, they found Ed in his
Cherokee on a Washington, D.C. street, smoke coming out of every
hole in his body. I didn't know whether to laugh or cry when I
noticed that I went to more funerals than parties this summer. I
didn't know whether to laugh or cry when I saw Edwin Jr. running
around the lobby, asking us why we were looking at his father sleep.
I think about El Barrio summers: running through the street like
there were no red lights. Ed's a cop. I'm a robber. Money was
something you asked an old-time hustler for so you could go to the
movies on Sunday. It wasn't suppose to kill you. I asked God to look
out for all of us—dead and alive. I walked home alone, refusing to
get high, and I thought how, if you looked close enough, you could
see a hole on Ed's forehead. I walked home, alone, refusing to get
high, thinking how my death will be just another reason why my boys
will pour beer on the street before they drink.

True Colors

you see
him now

grabbing me
around the neck

like I was his
son do this son do

that—flashing his
gold tooth whenever he

gets a chance
I might wear

dirty sneakers and
run to get his silk

shirts before the dry
cleaners close but I

remember we did
a bid together he

use to run and
cry on my shoulder like

he was my son do
this son do that

That night he went looking for
a poem
he left his electric typewriter humming
on the kitchen table
and ran out to the wide
sidewalks of Lenox Avenue

Aunties sat on their stoop box seats
mixing cheers and gossip
beers on the down low
With arms thrown to the sky
I celebrate a touchdown

A poet must look at the whole picture
One man's victory is stalked by another man's loss
The voice inside my head began to whisper:
> *Damn . . .*
> *One of them youngbloods might grow to*
> *be a poet in Harlem*
> *Or the little brother who caught the*
> *game-winning touchdown might have to*
> *sleep in the street one day*

That night he went looking for
a poem
he found two colors of love
A teenage couple embrace
by a bus-stop
I read his lips as they whisper
a sweet something into her smile
and that voice that never goes for a walk

comes to visit again:
> *I hope*
> *their dreams*
> *come true*

In one ear and it stood
as the poet turned the corner
He bumped into an ancient argument
Two fallen angels with scratched throats
pull and push each other
Ain't enough for both of them to
get high tonight
Use to be
he would serenade her
under a clear moonlight
and that voice meets
him in front of the liquor store:
> *Ain't no room for kissin' and huggin'*
> *In the middle of the night*
> *When luck is hard to find*

The poet came back to his
kitchen table with the last
voice that sounded like the blues
so he turned the electric hum into
this poem:
> *Show me a woman*
> *who is strung out on love*
> *I want to support*
> *her habit*

are rarely ever
sent to me

hanging off a broken stick
a dull red, white and blue flag—
one star instead of fifty—blows
in a hot breeze of bullet beans

congas y timbales bingbangbongboom
down the block and back; our blood
stands on its toes and we start to dance

winos lean over their canes and begin
a different story with the same ending:
"Geronimo wasn't shit compared to Papo"

chickens, rats, rabbits and cats are
tired of walking on broken-glass gardens;
they wait for the city to come and knock all
the gates down

once in a full blue moon rising above
crumbling gray rooftops I see a morenito
sitting on a stoop, licking the melting pineapple
ice off his palms

the violent revolutions of red and white police
sirens upset the sky blue peace of neon crucifixions

slow orange and yellow bulbs race around the
rims of stained bodega canopies. Hiding from the
rain, Old Man Jimmy sings the blues

postcards of El Barrio
are rarely ever sent to me

Harlem Plays the Best Ball in the World

I've heard all the stories
about the black magicians
performing on courts
where you had to come
with your own tricks
if you wanted to play

I've heard all the stories
about the days destroyed
by a white horse that came
galloping through the Harlem village
Summer night stories
when fun was a game won
and then a turn-out-the-lights set
let's rub a little kiss a little
we only got today forever, baby—
so can I have this dance

I've heard all the stories
about these legends
like The Goat who could
dunk twice in a single bound
Or the sound of Helicopter
rising to snatch a stack of
quarters off the top of
the backboard
And The Destroyer
who couldawouldashoulda
had a sneaker named after him

But the corner had more money
than the court

and after the game
it was time to get paid

We could blame
our mothers
fathers
rain
snow
blow
broken homes
but the legends
I heard about
rode express trains to games
where players pay with blood
and die without a pot to piss in

Monkey in the Middle

for Edmund Perry, Jr.

When you finally
got mad
it was too
late

You tried hard
to find
a space
where you could
be you
and not
get caught

Jumping
ducking
twisting
dashing
you died
not knowing
which one to
do next

My heart
use to beat
like yours
I use to be
the monkey
in the middle

If you was cute
they called you
Curious George

If you was ugly
they called you
King Kong
But once a monkey
always a monkey

Prep school pals in New Hampshire say
they just love you and yell:
    "Dance for us, Eddie! We think you're the coolest, man!"

Boys back on the block look at you angry and
they check you one time:
    "Damn, Ed. You been around them white boys too long, brother.
    You done lost all the ditty in your bop."

One day I
caught the ball
and threw it away
And then I told them
    I know
    who I am
    I know
    where I'm from
    And I ain't got no
    time to be playing
    games

There were tears waiting to
explode after Billie said,

"Thank you ladies and gentlemen."
The hearts of women sank into

the pain of why did her man do
her the way he did and not have to

explain. It didn't matter now that
he was home, she would say.

I will always remember the words:
I love you. I'm the man who will

be waiting for the explosion with
my hands cupped below your face.

Dreaming, I Was Only Dreaming

My history professor
has a bad habit
of looking at me when
discussing slavery

I can't relate
to fields of slaves
making America

I can hear the cries

beautiful and strong

All the facts are lies

Right or wrong
I raise my hand
to ask a question:
Professor
Why do you
keep looking at me
when you
discuss slavery
Last I heard
I was free

I was free. The sheriff untied the noose around my neck and I ran to grab the sun that was sitting on top of the mountain. I slipped off a cliff and before I could close my eyes I landed in front of a white mansion. An old lady sat on her rocking chair, swigging on a bottle of whiskey, making me dance with shots from her rifle. She laughed like a drunken hyena while the whole world sat in a movie theater, watching.

I snatched the rifle from her wrinkled hands and ran toward the crossroads. Before I could blink I was running through a jungle, trying to avoid the skeletons that were dangling off the trees and laughing like the old lady. Even the insects that were feeding on leftovers were giggling. By accident, I stepped on a baby's skull and swore to God that I would give my life to him if he let me out the jungle—alive.

I escaped from a box that had no light and found a black and white photograph sailing in the wind. It was my grandmother. She was crying as my battalion marched past the New York Public Library on 42nd Street and Fifth Avenue. The stone lions started laughing like the old lady when we stopped to salute the flag. The soldiers stood at attention when I walked through the front entrance of Charlie's Diner. I asked for a menu and the waitress threw a pot of boiling coffee on my face. The crowd cheered and continued flinging their confetti. America was blessed.

A gunshot made the crowd scatter. Everyone ran to the train station to see the policeman who was drowning in a pool of blood that kept oozing out of the hole in his forehead. The chief of police held a news conference on the steps of City Hall. He held my hand up like a boxer who just won a championship. He told the crowd that I was the one who shot the policeman. (Or someone who looked like me. He really couldn't tell because they were all wearing black berets, sunglasses and carrying automatic rifles. "Even the bullets were black" he cried as they escorted him to Bellevue Psychiatric Clinic.)

I held out my fist between the cage bars, raising my arm high like I wanted to ask a question. Blood dripped down my cheeks from a cut I had on my forehead. The policeman swam out of the blood pool and called my name. He wiped his red neck and smiled with his yellow teeth. Then he said, "Get up, boy. This ain't no dream. It's time to see the judge."

—One day a little girl asked me if I wrote love poems. I said, Yes. I use to write infinite I-love-you-and-never-want-to-lose-you poems. But now I write about scabs that chip off stone faces and fall on bleeding streets and I think all the poems I write are love poems. But the little girl wanted to hear a poem that sounds like the note you pass while the teacher's not looking. The kind that says, "I love you with ALL my heart. Do you love me? Yes or no? Pick one." So the next day I came back with notes for a Harlem love poem.

I am the poet of El Barrio. She is the princess of Harlem. We are strolling along Morningside Avenue, stopping occasionally to look over the gates of Morningside Park looking at the bright avenues and buying blocks with our dreams. The air feels like a cool bed sheet on a sticky summer night. Langston took his gal and wrapped her up in a neon dress and jukebox love songs. I turn my woman's face into a star so she can watch me walk down 125th Street.

We stop for ice cream. I get cherry-vanilla. The princess gets butter-pecan. In between licks we look at each other like now it's time to go home because so far it's been a beautiful day in the village and we ready to make love on the living room couch in our 18th floor project apartment, where we can keep the shades rolled up, feel the sunshine and let the Harlem River breeze soothe us to sleep. Lips and fingers are synchronized, soft bites and long moans make the peeping-tom pigeons sing. I am the type of poet who thinks that glory is the roar of boys and girls let out to the playground for recess; here they come, here we come, our first explosion makes the birds fly away. We got the spot and the sun is setting. Que rico tu eres, mami. This poem will end where it began: a man and his woman, a woman and her man, in love, on a beautiful day in the village of Harlem.

The New Stuff

for Bob Holman

Where's the new stuff, Willie?

The new stuff
is old
and improved
the shit
I be
writing about
the 'hood
the block
the Ave.
the corner
my boys
la vida
del pobre
no more doo-wop
over a can of fire
now it's cop-n-bop
tryin' to get higher
and keep warm
at the same time
　　　Know what I'm sayin', Bob?

The new stuff
is old
and improved
the shit
I be writing
about

Hustler's Song

Every morning
on my way to school
I hear the
hustler's song
  Coke-n-dope
  Dope-n-coke
  Yellow top cracks
  Black is out
  Purple! Purple!
  Dueces! How many? Got plenty!
  50, 60, 90 milligrams
  What's up, pa-pa? Whatchu need?
  Sets-n-points
  Loose joints
  Got it good, money . . .
  Walk me by and you won't get high
  If I'm lyin', I'm dyin'
  But don't come back cryin'

After the song
my heart
does a solo
subway roars underground
it's the sound
of death's
sunken cheeks
bloodshot eyes
blistered lips
rushing to work

Steppin' on the train
the folded crusty palms

of a tired construction worker
is the first thing I see

His eyes are closed
a moment of silence
a prayer for the strong
who are supposed to get stronger
by any means necessary

Damn . . .
building a skyscraper
is easier than building a family
Tomorrow
a brick might fall
on his head
or the boss
might be forced
to fire him
and make room
for a distant cousin

The baby needs formula
the rent got to be paid
and the man with the
tired hands
might have to start
singing the
hustler's song

Dear Petey:

Your wake was crowded, kid. We sent the biggest wreath to Farenga's. A giant red and white ribbon with T.C.B. across the middle. Your mother was grateful but now her days would be spent looking out the window, chain-smoking, and remembering how you use to run home from school, ready to look at cartoons. Eddie Ed heard her tell her friends "My Petey would still be alive if he wasn't always hanging out with those hoodlums from Lexington Avenue." After the funeral all our mothers went to your mother's house and they said prayers for nine nights straight, to make sure your spirit was safe when it reached the gates.

People who said that they loved you and that you were cool did not know that your real name was Pedro and that you were only 18 years old. We waited until every one paid you respects and then all twenty-five of us, strictly *The Crazy Bunch* way, walked up to your casket and one by one we kissed your cold blue face and locked your soul in our hearts. After that we went to the benches in Jefferson to get high in your name. We started to remember why we loved you. We imitated your walk that we could spot from three blocks away: that quick zig-zagging bop and your arms slashing the air as you tried to remember your newest rhyme. If you were talking to yourself that meant that you were trying to memorize the telephone number of a fly mami you just met on the train. "I'm in love, yo. For real this time."

When it was my turn to remember you I came up with the "data entry dream." Remember that night you came up to me and said: "Papo Love! What's up, baby? Yo, Pop, you know about data entry? It's good money in that. It got to be cuz it's with computers and if you know how to fuck with computers you definitely gonna get paid.

I'm going for an interview for that tomorrow. I got to go, kid. I ain't gonna be scrambling for the rest of my life. I got the number for this training program in the train. You know those signs they be having for shit like Planned Parenthood, those Julio y Marisol AIDS novellas, Jennifer Convertibles and shit like that? That's where I got it. You should come with me, Pop."

Slick Vic remembered the night you promised to be the first New Yurican rap star:

> Deep beneath my heart
> where there ain't no room to bite
> I'm a pure Porta-Reecan
> running fast against the night
> My pockets stay full
> and that ain't no bull
> Cuz my name is Pedro
> And I'm on the payroll
> Go Pedro! Get busy!
> Go Petey! Get busy!

And the whole avenue would start dancing and singing "Go Petey! Go Petey!" as you danced like a drunken joker with the lamppost as your spotlight.

I pour beer on the spot where Carlos and Marc left their tears; where they found you gasping for air, asking for some love just one more time. "You love me right fellas? Right, Los? Right, Marc?" And in unison they said: "Yeah, Pete. You know we love you, kid. Be a trooper, Pete. The ambulance is coming right now—no, no, no! Peteyyyy!" And that was enough for you to leave in peace.

After the city morgue bagged you up I wrote your birth and death dates inside the outline of your body. The white spray paint fades with every season. I cross myself every time I walk by because one night I might die on the same ground that I spit on.

I wake up early on Sundays and wait for the rainbows you send to the block. Davi saw one last week and said: "Yo, Pop, look! That's Petey telling us that he's all right, right?"

That was you right, Pete?

Saturday night
I'm on the 8:40
to New Rochelle
and points North
I'm running away
with my woman
running away from
El Barrio, New York City
Fast playing games
symbolic names
Slick Rick
Big Money D.
Hey you!
Who me?
Yeah, you.
Red light, green light, 1, 2, 3
Red light, green light, 1,2,3,
On the green—WALK
On the red—DON'T WALK
Stop! Freeze! Don't run.
Cuz you might get shot
for looking like
the wrong Black man
And whatever you do
please
please
don't sniff dope
three days in a row

Train is ready
steam whispers

a slow drag
out of Grand Central
through dark tunnels
where foot-long rats
swim in puddles
of leftover rain
Tanisa
my woman
lays her head
on my shoulder
I'm suppose
to be here
I'm doing the
right thing

Like a bullet
the iron horse
will shoot out of
the hole
on 98th Street and Park Avenue
We never see
how the rich really live
with gardens
in the middle of
the street
Doormen hailing taxis
in the rain
for poodles in
custom-made shearlings

Soon we'll see
where I'm from

I can never forget this panorama
of the other Park Avenue
Papo's Park Avenue
sounds like
a million hands
clapping in guaguanco time
Elevator in my stomach
where I stash
my dark secrets
starts to rise
I'm ready to get off
on 125th Street
so I could dive
into those hands

The streets
can kill you—
it's true
Clanging cuchifrito pots
compassionate curses ricochet off ho' row
my muses are calling, baby
I got to go
Forget our weekend in New Rochelle
Sunday paper
bagel brunch
sleeping in
after loving all night
Home is where I like to
find myself
when it's cold

110th Street
History of El Barrio, Spanish Harlem
salsa street legends
manteca bombs
many a bad muthafucka
done laughed and cried
ran and died
in the swollen arms
of this street
life and death
Boricuas in Nueva York
celebrate with this song
forever
para siempre, mami
para siempre

116th Street
LA MARQUETA is glittering
I don't need books
My culture
My history
is in the aisles
of bacalaito
ajecito
sofrito
pulpo
mi pana
I stretch my neck
to see
if I see

mi panas
Carlito y Marc
walking toward Madison Avenue
to buy a bag
half-n-half
for the rest of the night
awwwright!
a dripping leak-leaky bag
of Purple Rain
so that we can tranquilize
our souls
time
confusion
heartbreak
and get blind
Is that me
I see?
looking for a familiar dance
to a warm hip-hop boogie
writing a mad poem
to a sad beat
because the guns we play with
don't squirt water
or make that simulated machine gun rattle

Tanisa is sleeping now
she might be dreaming
about happy we gonna be
If it wasn't for her
my girl

my woman
my wifey
my main flame
my baby
always and forever
with a kiss
from Harlem
moreno Harlem
same beat
like my Barrio
soul y salsa
if it wasn't for her
I would be standing on the corner
thinking about the world
drinking blackberry brandy
keeping a cold hustler company
with stories from back in the days

   "Damn, Papo. Things ain't like they use to be . . ."

125th Street
Harlem, USA
I'm ready to jump off
before the doors close
have a nice day
and if this poem is too long
I really don't give a fuck
Because my heart is beating
and I'm alive
You know what I'm sayin'?
Can you hear my muses, Tanisa?

Shhhh . . .
I could tell her that I got some business to take care of
but she'll look at me with those sleepy eyes and that
soft voice and she'll say:
        "I am your business, Will."
And that's it—
Apollo Theater to the West
Willis Avenue Bridge to the East
A river waiting at each end of the boulevard
Poets and dead gangsters
chillin' at the bottoms
Nothing for me to do but jump
or turn back
cuz it ain't my time yet

I close my eyes and clench my teeth
I ask my grandmother's spirit for the strength to say no
I kiss Tanisa
careful not to shake her awake from her dreams

Doors close
steam whispers
a slow drag
away
I'm running away
with my woman
and I can't turn back
the El Barrio
Harlem night
is no longer mine

Acknowledgments

I want to send a shout-out full of love and respect to those people who were there before, during, and after the making of this book.

Gracias to Jill Bialosky for bringing my book to the table and making one of my dreams come true. To all the folks at the Nuyorican Poets Cafe for letting me share (especially Julio who I know wanted to kick my ass more than once but let his love get in the way). Props to T.C.B. (The Crazy Bunch)—the only fraternity I ever joined. I know "The Mad Poet of Harlem" Ed Randolph is sitting somewhere like a proud papa cuz he taught Papo how to fight with words. To the folks at Friends Seminary, Ithaca College, and CCNY where I became a protégé and learned how to keep a journal and have confidence in myself and my work (it all started when I walked into the office of Raymond Patterson and he said "I was thinking about you. . . . I know this literary agent . . . she's looking for an assistant . . .). The rest as they say is the story that must be told and it was the last time I called Marie "Ms. Brown." In the darkest of days there's always hope.

Because I fear forgetting that one person who played a small but significant role in this story, I will not make a "list" here. But I am confident that "my peeps" know who they are and how much space is reserved for them in mi corazon. One love to all of you.

And, above all, I want to give praise to Papa Dio for keeping my card in the deck—so far . . .

Some of these poems were last seen in the following publications: *Flare: The City Sun Literary Supplement, Bomb, A Gathering of the Tribes, New York Newsday, Longshot, In the Tradition, Aloud!, Young Tongues,* and *Boricuas.*

Palante mi panas . . .